W9-AAI-382

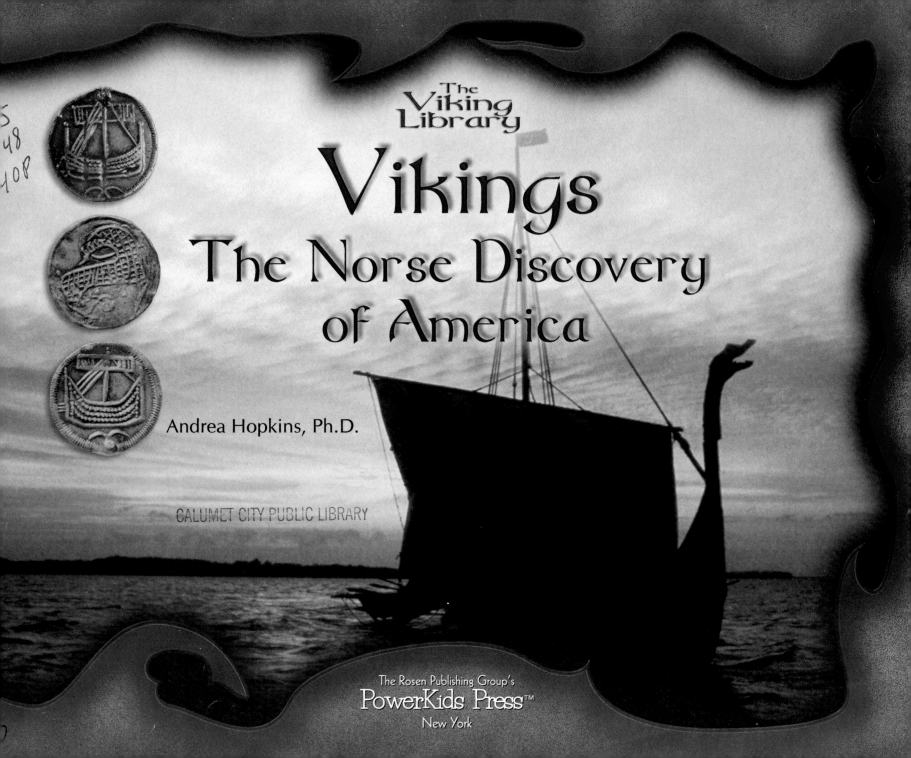

The
Viking
Library

Vikings
The Norse Discovery of America

Andrea Hopkins, Ph.D.

The Rosen Publishing Group's
PowerKids Press™
New York

To my husband Paul Reilly
Oh my America! My New-found-land!
How blest am I in this discovering thee!

Published in 2002 by The Rosen Publishing Group, Inc.
29 East 21st Street, New York, NY 10010

Copyright © 2002 by The Rosen Publishing Group, Inc.

First Edition

Book Design: Michael Caroleo

Project Editor: Frances E. Ruffin

Photo Credits: Title page (coins) © Werner Forman Archive; title page (longship) © Ted Spiegel/CORBIS; contents page and p. 15 © AKG Photo London; p. 4 © Bettmann/CORBIS; p. 7 (Faroe Islands) © Símun V. Arge; pp. 7 (both maps), 15 (map), 20 (map) prepared by Marcia Bakry, NMNH; pp. 8, 11 (Ingstads) © National Geographic; p. 11 (ruins) © William W. Fitzhugh, NMNH; pp. 12 (sod house), 20 (L'Anse aux Meadows) © Peter Harholdt, NMNH; p. 12 (jasper stones) © K.C. Kratt, BMS; p. 16 (East Greenland) © Judith Lindbergh; pp. 16 (Leif Eriksson), 19 (all) © North Wind Pictures.
Images on pp. 7, 11 (ruins), 12, 15 (map), 20 courtesy of the Artic Studies Center, Smithsonian National Museum of Natural History

Hopkins, Andrea.
Vikings : the Norse discovery of America / Andrea Hopkins.— 1st ed.
    p. cm. — (The Vikings library)
Includes index.
ISBN 0-8239-5817-5
1. America—Discovery and exploration—Norse—Juvenile literature. 2. North America—Discovery and exploration—Norse—Juvenile literature.
3. Vikings—North America—History—Juvenile literature. [1. Vikings. 2. North America—Discovery and exploration—Norse.] I. Title. II. Series.
E105 .H75 2002
970.01'3-dc21

00-012302

Manufactured in the United States of America

Contents

Before Christopher Columbus

This is the story of the first Europeans to find North America. Most people think Christopher Columbus, in 1492, was first. He wasn't. Columbus never set foot on the mainland of North America. The first Europeans to do so got there almost 500 years before him! Those people were Vikings. The Vikings came from Norway, Sweden, and Denmark, countries known today as **Scandinavia**. Vikings loved to explore new lands, and if they could, to settle down and live in them. During the Viking Age, from about A.D. 793 to A.D. 1050, thousands of Norse people left their native countries to seek wealth. Sometimes that wealth was in the form of stolen treasure, and sometimes it was in the form of good land to settle.

◀ *Vikings put fierce dragon-head carvings on the fronts of their ships when they were attacking other ships. Anyone who saw a ship like this coming toward him could expect no mercy.*

Across the North Atlantic

Most of Greenland was covered in ice. On the south and west coasts, there was some good land for farming. Erik built himself a big farm called Brattahlid, and in A.D. 986, he persuaded several hundred people to leave Iceland to settle in the new country.

Vikings started **communities** wherever they went. They went from Kiev in Ukraine to Greenland in the west. Slowly but surely, they traveled westward across the North Atlantic. In about A.D. 870, Vikings discovered Iceland. It was a large and almost empty island in the middle of the North Atlantic. Thousands of Norse people from Scandinavia went to live there. Within 60 years, all of the good farming land in Iceland was taken. In about A.D. 982, a man named Erik the Red was **exiled** from Iceland for killing someone. He sailed west and discovered a new land. He called it Greenland.

The top map of Iceland shows 393 years of settlements. The bottom map shows early Viking voyages to the Faroe Islands in the North Sea. A view of the sea from the Faroe Islands is in the background.

ARCTIC CIRCLE   18 W   Grimsey

WEST FIORDS   Eyja Fiord

Godafoss

Breiða Fjord   Hlar   EAST FIORDS
                    1700c

Western Quarter   North ern Quarter   Iceland

Faxafli c. 900   Southern   Eastern Quarter   Eastern
site of first Thing   Quarter   Vatnajökull   Horn
                  930 Allthing established   Western
                  at Thingvellir   Horn
                  1056
            Reykjavik   Skalholt   H
c. 873   K
Ingolf makes
permanent
settlement   c. 872

Davis Strait   Greenland   NORWEGIAN   Arctic Circle   Sweden
                                              SEA
                                                                          Norway
                                            Iceland   c. 870
Brattahlid   c.860   c.800
                                    Faeroes Is.
                                    Shetland Is.   c.800
                                    Orkney Is.   NORTH SEA
                            Hebrides   Scotland
          ATLANTIC OCEAN

——— Early voyages
——— Erik the Red, 985
- - - Sea ice limit

Icelandic Sagas

The Icelandic **sagas** are stories about the history and deeds of the people of Iceland. Two of the sagas, called The Greenlanders' Saga and Erik the Red's Saga, tell how Greenland was **colonized**. They also describe how the Vikings discovered and explored a small part of North America. These sagas were written down in the early 1200s, at least 200 years after the Viking voyages to North America took place. The sagas tell of four separate **voyages** made by members of Erik the Red's family, from about A.D. 1000 to about A.D. 1010. These stories had been passed down for 200 years by people telling them to one another, and there is a lot of **fiction** mixed in with the facts.

◄ *The map shows the Viking voyages and explorations described in Icelandic sagas. Often during long winter nights these stories were passed down from one person to another.*

Ruins at L'Anse aux Meadows

Many modern historians did not believe that the Vikings really had reached North America as early as A.D. 1000. They said the events recorded in the two sagas about Greenland must be made up. Then in 1960, a Norwegian explorer, Helge Ingstad, and his **archaeologist** wife, Anne Stine Ingstad, discovered and **excavated** the site of a Norse settlement on the northern tip of the island of Newfoundland in Canada. This proved beyond doubt that the stories told in the sagas were at least partly true. At L'Anse aux Meadows, the Ingstads discovered the remains of three large longhouses and five smaller buildings. Since the discovery, many teams of archaeologists have sifted patiently through the earth, **peat**, and garbage dumps at the site and have made some amazing discoveries.

L'Anse aux Meadows (large photo), *site of a Norse settlement, was explored by Helge and Anne Stine Ingstad* (top right).

History in a Midden

Archaeologists can find out a lot about people by examining their garbage! Norse people used to put all of their household waste into a pit, called a midden. The middens at L'Anse aux Meadows were small, so the site was lived in for only a few years. At the time of the settlement, around A.D. 1000, there were no Native American people living in that area. The Norse people who lived in these houses left many things behind, including a collection of "fire-starters" made of a special kind of stone, called jasper. Many wood chips and nail fragments showed that metalworking and carpentry were done there. A needle, part of a spindle, and loom weights showed that at least one woman had lived nearby. None of the buildings had been used for housing animals.

◄ Bottom: *This is a rebuilt Viking mud hut at L'Anse aux Meadows.*
   Top: *Many pieces of a stone called jasper were found there.*

Leif the Lucky

Leif came to a second land that had thick forests and miles of beach. Leif called this place Forest Land. It was probably the coast of Labrador in Canada. The long, white, sandy beach the Norse called Wonder Beach was probably Porcupine Strand in Southern Labrador.

In the late summer of A.D. 986, a man named Bjarni tried to sail to Greenland from Iceland. His ship was blown off course. When the stormy weather cleared, Bjarni saw a strange coastline with thick forests and open meadows. Bjarni knew this was not Greenland, so he didn't land. He changed course and that time reached Greenland. He told other people about the new land he had seen. Leif the Lucky, a son of Erik the Red, bought Bjarni's ship. Leif hired a crew of 35 men, and they set sail for the west in A.D. 1000. They sailed for three days and saw a flat, rocky land. Leif called this place Slab Land. This land may have been Baffin Island.

The painting of Leif the Lucky, also known as Leif Eriksson, shows him sailing to North America. Top: This is a map of the routes that Leif and his brother Thorvald took to North America.

VINLAND

MARKLAND

N

Gulf of Saint Lawrence

Prince
Edward Is.

Kjalarnes
(Keel Point)

Nova Scotia

Krossanes
(Cross Point)

Newfoundland

Thorvalds first summer
Thorvalds second summer
Leifs explorations
Leifsbuðir
(Leif's camp)

Vinland

Leif and his crew sailed southwest until they reached a land of forests and **fertile** meadows. They decided to stay there for the winter. One group of men went off to explore the new land, while the others worked at the base. Leif divided his men into two parties. The Greenlanders' Saga tells us that a German man named Tyrkir found wild grapevines. Wine was a **luxury** in Europe. The Vikings could gain wealth by having their own source of grapes to make wine. Because of the grapevines, Leif decided to call that country Vinland, meaning "Wineland."

◄ *Today Greenland is covered with ice and glaciers. Norse people no longer live there. The small painting shows Leif Eriksson and his men exploring Vinland.*

The Skraelings

The sagas tell us that a man called Thorfinn Karlsefni and his wife, Gudrid, decided to start a permanent **settlement** in Vinland. They took 60 men and five women, and many animals and goods. They met some people who were already living in Vinland. These people were Native Americans. Because they looked strange to the Vikings, the Vikings called the people Skraelings, which means "uglies." At first the two groups got along well, though they spoke different languages. The Skraelings brought furs to trade with the Vikings for milk, cheese, and red cloth. Later there was conflict between the Vikings and the Skraelings.

This painting shows Thorfinn and Gudrid Karlsefni landing in Vinland.

This painting shows Freydis Eriksdaughter, the sister of Leif Erikksson, fighting the Skraelings.

Quebec

VINLAND

Land of the
One-Legged People

Bjarney
(Bear Island)

Hóp (Tidal Pool)
(New York)

Straumfjord
(Stream Fjord)

Gulf of Saint Lawrence

Straumsey
(Stream Island)

Newfoundland

Nova Scotia

Furðustrandir
(Wonder Strand)

N

Karlsefni
Gudrid and Karlsefni
Karlsefni
Thorhall

Meadows of Mystery

There are some big differences between what the sagas told about Vinland and what was found at L'Anse aux Meadows. The sagas say wild grapes and wild wheat grew at Hop, Thorfinn and Gudrid Karlsefni's settlement. Hop was on the shore of a **tidal** lake, so ships could enter only at high tide. The Karlsefnis brought farm animals with them, including cows and a bull. Native Americans lived at Hop. At L'Anse aux Meadows, however, archaeologists found that at the time of the Viking settlement there were no Native Americans nearby. It was also too far north for cattle, sheep, or even fruit such as wild grapes to survive. There must have been two settlements. Hop most describes the Miramichi Bay area in New Brunswick. Maybe the ruins of Hop are still there, waiting to be discovered.

◄ *This image at L'Anse aux Meadow was a site of a Viking settlement in Newfoundland. Top: The map shows the places where Thorfinn Karlsefni and his men explored on Vinland.*

What Became of the Greenlanders?

An eleventh-century coin was dug up in Maine. A stone arrowhead was found near a Viking graveyard in Greenland. Some say that Native Americans carried the Norse off to slavery. Maybe the Norse sailed away to try their luck in Vinland.

As far as we know, the Vikings made no further attempts to start a colony on the mainland of North America. They did go back from time to time to get timber, grapes, and fur. The Greenlanders last were seen alive in 1424. By 1721, both settlements were long-deserted ruins. Archaeologists know that in Greenland the weather grew colder, food became scarce, and people died more easily of the cold or disease. The Norse colony survived for 500 years and then disappeared without a trace. It is one of the great unsolved mysteries of the Middle Ages.

Glossary

archaeologist (ar-kee-AH-luh-jist) Someone who studies the life and culture of the past, especially by studying artifacts.

colonized (KAH-luh-nyzd) Having settled in a new land and claimed it for the government of another country.

communities (kuh-MYOO-nih-teez) Groups of people or animals that live in the same place.

excavated (EK-skuh-vayt-ed) To have dug up something that was buried or covered by rocks.

exiled (EG-zyld) To have made a person leave his or her home or country as a punishment.

fertile (FUR-tul) Good for making and growing things.

fiction (FIK-shun) Something that is made up through imagination, such as a story.

luxury (LUK-shuh-ree) Something that is nice or expensive but is not really needed.

peat (PEET) A kind of plant material that is used in fires for heat or cooking.

sagas (SAH-guz) Stories about the history and experiences of a people; the stories are written down after being passed from one generation to another by telling aloud.

Scandinavia (scan-dih-NAY-vee-a) Northern Europe, usually Norway, Sweden, and Denmark.

settlement (SEH-tul-ment) A small village or group of houses.

tidal (TY-dul) Relating to the tides of a body of water.

voyages (VOY-ih-jez) Journeys by water.

Index

B
Bjarni, 14

C
Columbus, Christopher, 5

E
Erik the Red, 6, 9, 14
Erik the Red's saga, 9

G
Greenland, 6, 9, 14, 22
Greenlanders' saga, 9

I
Iceland, 6, 9, 14
Ingstad, Anne Stine, 10
Ingstad, Helge, 10

K
Karlsefni, Guidrid, 18, 21
Karlsefni, Thorfinn, 18, 21

L
L'Anse aux Meadows, 10, 13, 21
Leif (the Lucky), 14, 17

N
Native American(s), 13, 18, 21
Newfoundland, Canada, 10
North America, 5, 9, 10, 22

S
Scandinavia, 5, 6
Skraelings, 18

V
Vinland, 17, 18, 21

Web Sites

To learn more about the Vikings, check out these Web sites:
http://www.control.chalmers.se/vikings/viking.html
http://home.ringnett.no/bjornstad/index.html